MAKING AND BREAKING CODES

MAKING SECRET CODES

BY JILLIAN GREGORY

Consultant:
Professor Mihir Bellare
Department of Computer Science and Engineering
University of California, San Diego

CAPSTONE PRESS
a capstone imprint

Edge Books are published by Capstone Press,
151 Good Counsel Drive, P.O. Box 669, Mankato, Minnesota 56002.
www.capstonepub.com

Printed in the United States of America in North Mankato, Minnesota.
032010
005740CGF10

Books published by Capstone Press are manufactured with paper
containing at least 10 percent post-consumer waste.

Library of Congress Cataloging-in-Publication Data
Gregory, Jillian.
Making secret codes / by Jillian Gregory.
    p. cm.—(Making and breaking codes)
Includes bibliographical references and index.
Summary: "Discusses different methods for creating secret codes"—Provided
by publisher.
ISBN 978-1-4296-4567-6 (library binding)
1. Cryptography—Juvenile literature. 2. Ciphers—Juvenile literature. I. Title.
II. Series.
Z103.3G74 2011
652'.8—dc22   2010004161

EDITORIAL CREDITS

Mandy Robbins, editor; Ted Williams, designer; Marcie Spence,
    media researcher; Laura Manthe, production specialist

PHOTO CREDITS

Alamy: North Wind Picture Archives, 11; Bettmann: Corbis, 14; Capstone Press:
cover, 24, Karon Dubke, 17, 26; Courtesy of the National Security Agency,
12; iStockphoto: diane39, 7; Monticello: photograph by Chad Wollerton, 27;
Newscom: 8, 16, 19, AFP Photo/Gabriel Bouys, 28 (left), David Griffin/Icon
SMI, 4, Shelly Castellano Icon SMI, 23; Peter Newark Historical Pictures:
The Bridgeman Art Library, 15; Shutterstock: MalibuBooks, 5; Fotocrisis, 21;
Wikimedia/Wiso, 28 (right)

TABLE OF CONTENTS

CODES ALL AROUND US

Have you ever seen a stock car race? The race cars speed around a track at dangerously high speeds. Stock car officials use a code of different colored flags to communicate with drivers on the track. A yellow flag means caution. A white flag means there is one more lap left in the race.

Yellow flags are waved when there is an accident on the track.

You may not be a stock car driver, but you also use codes every day. You use an area code when you make a long-distance phone call. You use a zip code when you write a mailing address. Some people use a shorthand code when they text.

"TTYL" is shorthand for "Talk to you later."

These codes are meant to make communication easier. But what if you only want certain people to know what you're trying to communicate? You can use cryptography to write messages in a secret code. Read on for some code-making tips and tricks.

CODE FACT

Even the grades your teachers give you are a type of code. Different letters tell how well you're doing in your classes.

CHAPTER 1

BREAKING DOWN CRYPTOGRAPHY

Cryptography is all about codes. Codes mask messages so that only the people who understand the code can read the message.

A secret message is **encoded** by changing plain text into coded text. The code maker uses a specific process known as the key. The key tells you how to change the code to plain text.

Some codes replace words or letters with different words or letters. Numbers or symbols could also represent letters or words in a code. A codebook can be used as a key to this type of code. But when you use a codebook, all the information needed to **decode** your message is in one place. If someone finds your codebook, the secret is out! He or she can easily crack your code.

Write your messages in secret code to keep your notes private.

A more complex key could refer to a system or method for decoding a message. The more complex the method is, the more difficult your code will be to crack.

Sometimes a message is encoded by scrambling up the letters of the plain text. The key is to unscramble them in the proper way. These methods range from simple to incredibly complex.

encode—to turn ordinary language into coded language by using a key

decode—to turn something that is written in code into ordinary language

CODE METHODS

Most codes are created using one of two main methods. These techniques are **transposition** and **substitution**.

transposition—rearranging the order of items in something

substitution—using a symbol to represent something other than its original meaning

CODE FACT

In the 1600s, astronomers Johannes Kepler and Galileo used anagrams to record their scientific discoveries. The anagrams disguised the scientists' work until it was published. This stopped other scientists from stealing the information.

What do the words "ant," "tan," and "nat" have in common? They are the same three letters written in a different order. This group of words is an example of an anagram. An anagram is an example of a letter transposition code.

Using anagrams, you can rearrange the letters in your message. Mix up the letters in each word, or rearrange the entire sentence. Unscrambling an entire sentence is more difficult than unscrambling one word.

The following three anagrams represent the same sentence. The first line is the most difficult to crack. The second and third lines get easier.

Et nc awiry uotees c r sages me s.
Yu oanc wit re teecrs mags sees.
Oyu anc tewir creets gemessas.

☑ *See page 32 for answer.*

CHAPTER 2

CODES THROUGHOUT HISTORY

Codes have shaped world history in more ways than you could probably imagine. Scientists used codes to protect information. Military leaders have used codes during times of war. These codes were transmitted through writing, the telegraph, or radio.

CAESAR SHIFT CODE

In ancient Rome, Julius Caesar used a shift code to communicate with his generals. Each letter was shifted a set number to the right in the alphabet. This number was called the key number. Caesar's generals needed to know the key number to decode the secret message.

If the key number was four, the letter "A" would be written as "E." The letter "Z" would be written as "D." Unfortunately, the code was very simple to crack. It only took 25 guesses to decode—one for every letter of the alphabet that wasn't plain text.

Roman soldiers carried Caesar's secret messages to his generals during times of war.

Create your own Caesar shift code using 13 as the key number. Write out the alphabet in one line. Then write the alphabet again underneath the first line, but shift the letters 13 places. So "A" would be "N." When you get to the letter "Z," go back to "A." Now decode the message below using your Caesar shift code.

V yvxr lbhe arj onpxcnpx.

 *See page 32 for answer.*

UNION ROUTE CODE

Codes were also used during the Civil War (1861-1865). Union forces used a word transposition code called the Union Route code to send messages. These messages were sent using a telegraph. But this type of code is also fairly simple to crack. Once someone figured out the most common words, they could easily decode the message. To increase security, the code pattern and code words were changed 10 times during the Civil War. Only the code telegraph operators had access to these patterns and words.

The message was encoded and written in a grid of seven rows and five columns. The message was read up the first column and down the second. Then the reader would read up the fifth column, down the fourth, and then up the third.

Reading messages out of order makes codes harder to crack. Combine this trick with your Caesar shift code. To decode the message below, read it in the order you would read the Union Route code. Use your Caesar shift code to substitute letters.

F	G		E	H
V	E	P	B	
U	V	E	B	L
G	P	R	Q	R
R	X	U	R	X
F	G	T	G	N
H	B	H	B	Z

☑ See page 32 for answer.

NAVAJO CODE TALKERS

During World War II (1939–1945), the United States and Japan fought on different sides. Both countries tried to create secret codes. The U.S. military recruited American Indians from the Navajo tribe to create a secret code. The code used the Navajo language to send secret messages. The American Indian servicemen who used this code were called "Navajo code talkers."

Navajo code talkers sent their messages over radios.

The Navajo code consisted of 274 military words that had English code words. A Navajo code word was created for each English code word. Uncommon words were spelled out using Navajo language code words that represented letters. This code was so hard to crack, the Japanese never broke it throughout the war.

The Navajo language was never written down. Code talkers had to memorize the code.

You can take a tip from the Navajo code talkers by using code words from a different language. Say you're talking about your friend. Your code word for that person could be "cat." Translate "cat" into Spanish and you have *gato*. Even if someone knew *gato* meant "cat," they'd still have no idea who you were talking about.

CHAPTER 3

CODE PLAY

There's no limit to what you can do with codes. Even simple methods can create codes that baffle your friends and family. Combine several simple techniques, and your codes will be even trickier to crack.

CODE FACT

Leonardo daVinci used a mirror for one of his codes. He wrote text backward so that it could only be read in a mirror. Try writing your name backward and then hold the paper up to a mirror.

FOLDED SECRETS

Codes can be made by writing a message along the folds of a piece of paper. Fold a piece of paper **vertically** into fourths. Write the secret message down the folds. Fill in the rest of the note **horizontally** with another message. When the paper is unfolded, the secret message is hidden. To learn the secret, a person must know the key—fold the paper. You can make the code trickier to crack by only writing down two of the three folds.

CODEBOOK KEY

You can also make a codebook to create a secret code. Pictures, symbols, or numbers can disguise the meanings of letters or words. Only those who have the codebook will be able to decode the secret message.

The coded message is:

(<<@   (<   —{@<$ #?[&&)

Decode the message using the codebook below. What was the message?

A	B	C	D	E	F	G	H	I	J	K	L	M
—	/	?	>	<	{	}	[	]	=	+	)	(

N	O	P	Q	R	S	T	U	V	W	X	Y	Z
*	&	^	%	$	#	@	!	~	≜	⊙	λ	↗

☑ *See page 32 for answer.*

Samuel Morse

MORSE CODE

In the mid–1800s, Samuel Morse created a letter substitution code that was sent using a telegraph. A combination of dots and dashes represented each letter. Morse code is often used by people in emergencies. People in trouble will spell out "S.O.S." That is the international signal for "Help!"

In Morse code, "S" is represented by three dots, and "O" is represented by three dashes. The message "S.O.S." can be tapped out audibly or spelled visually. An audible message would sound like three short taps, followed by three long taps, and then three more short taps. A visual message would look like this: ... ——— ...

GREEK BOX CODE

The Greek box code uses number-letter substitution. Create a five-column, five-row grid as shown on the next page. The letter "Z" is not used very often, so it is left out. You could also leave out the letter "K" and use "C" to represent that sound.

ONE TIME PAD

Even complex codes have eventually been broken with the help of a computer. However, one very strong code uses the "one time pad" **algorithm**. The plain text and a secret key, known as the one time pad, are used to create the code. The key is used only one time. This key is the same length as the plain text message. Because the code is random and is never used more than once, it can't be cracked without the key. In the past, the one time key was written on a pad of paper. For increased security, the text was so small that the key could only be read using a magnifying glass.

algorithm—a process for solving a problem in a certain number of steps

Coded letters are written in pairs of numbers. The pair of numbers indicates the column and row where each letter is located. For example, the letter "B" is written as 21. The letter "R" is written as 34. To decode the message, locate the letter using the column and row indicated.

	1	2	3	4	5
1	A	B	C	D	E
2	F	G	H	I	J
3	K	L	M	N	O
4	P	Q	R	S	T
5	U	V	W	X	Y

Decode the message
using the Greek box code.

22 34 51 11 54   52 53 21

✓ *See page 32 for answer.*

GEOMETRIC CODE

A geometric code changes the order of the letters of the secret message. The letters are written following a grid of columns and rows. The key is the size and direction of the grid used to write the message. The code below is written in an eight-row by two-column grid. The message is read down instead of left to right.

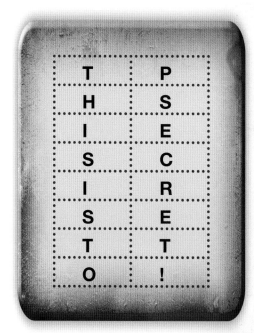

Write the encoded text using the horizontal pairs in the grid. The encoded text is TP HS IE SC IR SE TT O! Your friend can decode the message using a grid with two-columns and eight-rows.

BASEBALL CODES

Have you ever seen a baseball coach touch his nose and lift his hat? Baseball coaches communicate with players using a visual code. Players look for signs that tell them what to do. The rest of the signs are dummy signs. Dummy signs prevent other teams from figuring out the code.

You don't have to play baseball to have fun with a visual code. Tap your cheek, touch your elbow, and pull your earlobe. You and your friends could have a conversation without saying or writing anything!

As cryptography advanced, people built instruments to create more difficult codes. Two famous code instruments are the Scytale and the Alberti disk. You can build these instruments yourself.

THE SCYTALE

A Scytale is a long strip of paper wrapped around a rod. A message is written on the paper while it is wrapped around the rod. When the paper is unwound, it looks like a strip of random letters. A rod of the same size must be used to decode the message.

Build your own Scytale using a cardboard toilet paper roll. Cut a piece of paper into a long, thin strip. Wrap the paper around the toilet paper roll. Make sure the paper doesn't overlap and covers the toilet paper roll completely. Write the secret message across the roll. Remove the piece of paper from the toilet paper roll.

Give the piece of paper to your friends and family. See if they can figure out the secret message. When they give up, use the toilet paper roll to show them how to decode the message.

CODE FACT

A Scytale was used in ancient Greece to send secret messages during military battles. For more security, messages included a code. This code told the reader which size rod was needed to decode the message.

THE ALBERTI DISK

In the 1400s, Leone Battista Alberti created the Alberti disk. The Alberti disk has two alphabet wheels with the same center.

> To make your code more difficult to crack, reposition your Alberti disk after every 10 letters.

Try making your own Alberti disk. First, cut a circle out of cardboard. Then cut a larger circle out of cardboard. Write the alphabet in random order around the outer edges of both circles. Use a paper fastener to attach the two circles through the center.

Rotate the disks until the letter "A" on the inside disk matches up with a different letter on the outside disk. Keep the disks in the same position as you write your message.

See if your friends and family can figure out the secret message without the Alberti disk. Then show them how you set up the Alberti disk so they can decode the message. You can create hundreds of substitution codes using the Alberti disk.

JEFFERSON'S SECRET CODE

Thomas Jefferson was the third president of the United States. He needed a way to protect sensitive political information. Jefferson invented a wheel code that creates polyalphabetic codes. These codes use more than one alphabet at a time. The wheel code is made of 26 wooden wheels on an iron rod. The wheels are lined up a specific way to reveal the message. The United States Army used a version of Jefferson's wheel code in the early 1900s.

As long as people have been making codes, others have been trying to break them. Code breakers try to decode messages without knowing the key to the code. They look for patterns in the encoded text that could give them clues about how to crack it. The challenge to code makers is to stay one step ahead of those who would try to crack their codes.

CODE FACT

In May 1975, Stanford computer scientist Martin Hellman (right) and cryptographer Whitfield Diffie (left) created public-key cryptography.

PUBLIC-KEY CRYPTOGRAPHY

Cryptography throughout history was not always secure. Codes were created and decoded using the same key. Modern cryptography uses codes that are more secure than historic ones. These codes are all around us. When someone shops on an Internet Web site, he or she pays with a credit card. Modern codes are used to protect credit card information as it flows over the Internet. One method used is public-key cryptography. This form of cryptography uses a public key and a private key. The public key is used to encode the information. The public key can be used by anyone. The private key is used to decode information. The private key is kept secret.

Like modern cryptographers, you too can keep trying to create stronger codes. Start by using the techniques in this book. Then you can combine methods to make your code more difficult to crack. Keep at it, and perhaps someday you can join the ranks of today's top cryptographers.

GLOSSARY

algorithm (AL-guh-rih-thum)—a process for solving a problem in a certain number of steps

anagram (AN-uh-gram)—a secret message made by rearranging the letters in the original message

cryptography (krip-TAH-gruh-fee)—the study of secret writing, especially codes

decode (dee-KOHD)—to turn something that is written in code into ordinary language

encode (en-KOHD)—to turn ordinary language into coded language

horizontal (hor-uh-ZON-tuhl)—flat and parallel to the ground

polyalphabetic code (PAH-lee-al-fuh-bet-ik CODE)—a code that uses multiple alphabets

substitution (sub-stuh-TOO-shun)—using a letter, number, or symbol to represent something other than its original meaning

transposition (trans-puh-ZIH-shun)—rearranging the order of items in something

vertical (VUR-tuh-kuhl)—straight up and down

READ MORE

Becker, Helaine. *Secret Agent Y.O.U.: The Official Guide to Secret Codes, Disguises, Surveillance, and More!* Toronto: Maple Tree Press, 2006.

Gregory, Jillian. *Breaking Secret Codes.* Making and Breaking Codes. Mankato, Minn.: Capstone Press, 2011.

Lambert, David, and the Diagram Group. *Super Little Giant Book of Secret Codes.* New York: Sterling Pub. Co., 2007.

INTERNET SITES

FactHound offers a safe, fun way to find Internet sites related to this book. All of the sites on FactHound have been researched by our staff.

Here's all you do:

Visit *www.facthound.com*

Type in this code: 9781429645676

INDEX

☑ ANSWERS

PAGE 9: *You can write secret messages.*

PAGE 11: *I like your new backpack.*

PAGE 13: *Use this trick to make your code tougher.*

PAGE 18: *Meet me after school.*

PAGE 21: *Great job*